MW01247579

TRUD

JUNIOR
BIOGRAPHIES

Kathy Furgang

JUSTIN TRUDEAU

PRIME MINISTER OF CANADA

BUCKHAM MEMORIAL LIBRARY
FARIBAULT, MN 55021

Enslow Publishing
101 W. 23rd Street
Suite 240
New York, NY 10011
USA
enslow.com

WORDS TO KNOW

avalanche A large amount of snow that falls quickly down a mountainside.

cabinet A group of people who advise or guide an elected official.

campaign An effort to win an election or be voted to a particular task.

citizen A member of a community or nation.

indigenous Originally from a certain place.

prime minister An elected political leader of a country.

refugees People forced to leave their country in order to escape war or another crisis.

residence A place where someone lives.

volunteer A person who offers time or services to help others at no charge.

CONTENTS

Justin Trudeau

CHAPTER 1

A PRIME MINISTER'S SON

Canada's future **prime minister**, Justin Trudeau, was born on Christmas Day in 1971. He was the son of the nation's fifteenth prime minister, Pierre Trudeau. He and Justin's mother, Margaret, soon had two other sons, Alexandre and Michel.

The three Trudeau boys grew up in the **residence** of the prime minister. Their father was one of the longest-serving prime ministers in Canada. Childhood for Justin was not always easy. He lived in the public spotlight. When he was five years old, his parents separated and he and his brothers lived with his father.

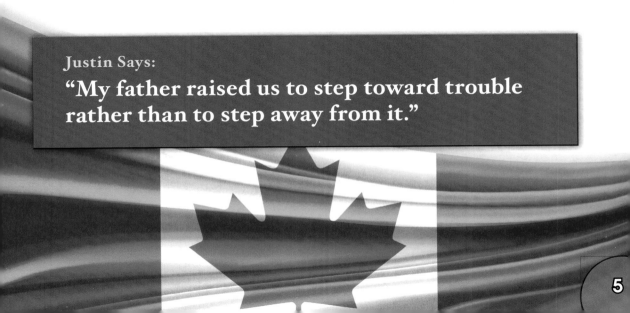

Justin Says:

"My father raised us to step toward trouble rather than to step away from it."

GROWING UP IN THE SPOTLIGHT

Young Justin is held by his mother, Margaret, in 1972.

Although Justin and his brothers grew up known to all people of Canada, their parents kept their lives mainly private. They were sent to both private schools and public schools during their times as students. Like many Canadians, they learned both English and French and could speak them both fluently.

In 1998, Justin's youngest brother, Michel, died in an avalanche at twenty-three years old. Justin later served on the board of the Canadian Avalanche Foundation to promote avalanche safety.

Prime minister Pierre Trudeau poses with his three sons (from left) Justin, Alexandre, and Michel in 1980.

Justin graduated from college in 1994 and soon decided to become a schoolteacher. He thought this would be a good way to have a positive influence on the world. He taught for years in Vancouver, on Canada's west coast. He taught both French and math.

CHAPTER 2
A BEGINNING IN POLITICS

In 2003, Justin began dating the woman he would marry, Sophie Grégoire. They were wed in 2005, and in the following years they had three children: Xavier, Ella-Grace, and Hadrien.

As Justin and Sophie were working on building their family, Justin worked on a career in public life. He spoke at conferences about youth issues and the environment. He encouraged people to do community service and volunteer.

The two opposing political parties in Canada are the Liberal Party and the Conservative Party.

Then Justin began to follow in his father's footsteps. He entered politics. He went out into the community and met many citizens. He explained his political ideas as a member of the Liberal Party.

A TRUSTED LEADER

Justin did more than just meet people. He listened to their concerns. He thought about how the government

In 2005, Justin married Sophie Grégoire. He first knew Sophie as a child, when she was his brother's classmate.

Justin gives an interview during his campaign for the Liberal Party in 2008.

Justin Says:

"Canadians are broad minded and big hearted, fair and honest, hard working, hopeful, and kind."

could help solve their problems. He invited other community leaders to listen to the citizens also. Justin felt that this was the best way to understand what needed to be done.

Justin ran for election in Papineau, a section of Montreal, Canada. After a lot of hard work, he won that leadership position. He continued to work hard and became known for his commitment to the people.

In 2012, Justin decided to run for prime minister. It would be difficult to campaign, but he hoped he could help lead the nation successfully.

CHAPTER 3
PRIME MINISTER OF CANADA

In 2015, after a hard campaign against his opponent, Justin was elected prime minister. He ran on some simple ideas for his political party. He wanted the middle class to grow and do well. He wanted to promote the freedom and diversity the nation has to offer.

Justin was sworn in as Canada's twenty-third prime minister on November 4, 2015. The prime minister's cabinet is a group of people working in the government. They advise the prime minister about different topics. Justin felt it was important to choose an equal number of men and women for his cabinet. He chose fifteen men and fifteen women. This was the first time in Canada's history that the cabinet represented such equality.

Justin Says:

"It's important to be here before you today to present to Canada a cabinet that looks like Canada."

Justin gives a speech shortly after being sworn in as Canada's twenty-third prime minister in 2015.

PRIME MINISTER OF THE PEOPLE

From the very first day Justin took office, people knew he would be a different type of prime minister. He did not arrive at his official residence, Rideau Hall, in the black cars that other politicians used. Instead, the entire Trudeau family arrived in a bus. They stopped to talk to the crowds that greeted them. They took selfies with them.

However, Justin understood that it was not only his supporters in the Liberal Party that he needed to

Justin, fifth from left in the front row, poses with his new cabinet in 2015.

serve. He needed to serve all Canadians. That included people of the opposing party. It included people whose needs had not been met. It included people of Canada's indigenous populations, too.

CANADA'S PLACE IN THE WORLD

As prime minister, Justin wants to strengthen Canada's role as a world leader. He travels the world meeting the heads of many other countries. He wants to make the world safe from terrorists. He wants to make sure people are responsible about the environment.

Justin enjoys outdoor sports. With Canada's cold weather, that includes snowboarding and skiing.

BUCKHAM MEMORIAL LIBRARY
FARIBAULT, MN 55021

Justin attends a 2017 summit with German leader Angela Merkel, US president Donald Trump, and Italian prime minister Paolo Gentiloni.

Justin also wants to make sure that Canada and the United States keep the friendly relationship they have always had. He works on all parts of the Canadian government. He knows he is an important role model to the people of his country.

CHAPTER 4
A ROLE MODEL

Justin knows he can help improve the lives of other people by doing the right thing. In 2015, Canada welcomed thousands of **refugees** into the country. The country of Syria was having a terrible crisis that left many people without homes. Justin not only allowed the refugees into his country, he greeted them personally. He went to the airport and handed out winter coats. He knew the people would need them as they came to the cold climate of Canada.

Even with the new refugees, he does not take personal credit. He thanks the citizens of his country: "It was because communities opened up their homes, their churches, their community centers. Everyone said, 'Let's do our part to give some people in a terrible situation a better future.'"

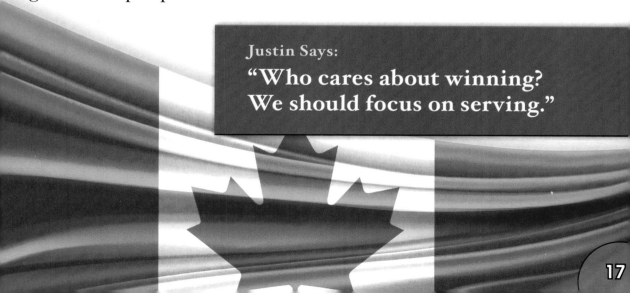

Justin Says:
"**Who cares about winning?
We should focus on serving.**"

The Trudeau family marches in the Vancouver Pride Parade in 2016 (from left, Xavier, Justin, Hadrien, Ella-Grace, and Sophie).

LEADING INTO THE FUTURE

Despite his many accomplishments, Justin knows there is still a lot he can do to help the nation. He is the second youngest prime minister and he is eager to make the government work for all its people.

Canada recently celebrated its 150th birthday. But Justin shares the concerns of many other Canadians. They do not want to ignore the population of indigenous

In 2007, Justin starred in a TV miniseries called *The Great War*. It told the story of Canada's role in World War I. He played the role of Talbot Papineau, a soldier from Quebec.

Justin speaks about Canada's promising future at a celebration for the country's 150th birthday.

people in the country. They lived on the land for centuries before it became known as Canada. He wants to serve their needs just as much as other Canadians'. Justin's thoughtful leadership can help bring Canada into the future.

Justin helps hand out coats to Syrian refugees in 2015.

TIMELINE

1971 Justin Pierre James Trudeau is born on December 25 in Ontario, Canada.

1977 Justin's parents separate.

1994 Graduates from McGill University in Montreal.

1998 Justin's brother Michel dies in an avalanche.

2005 Marries Sophie Grégoire.

2007 Stars in the TV miniseries *The Great War*.

2013 Wins election for the leadership of Canada's Liberal Party.

2015 Becomes twenty-third prime minister of Canada.

LEARN MORE

BOOKS

Blevins, Wiley. *Follow Me Around Canada.* New York, NY: Children's Press, 2017.

Bowers, Vivien. *Hey Canada!* New York, NY: Tundra Books, 2012.

National Geographic Kids. *Weird But True Canada: 300 Outrageous Facts About the True North.* New York, NY: National Geographic Kids, 2018.

WEBSITES

Canadian Geographic

www.canadiangeographic.ca/content/kids-games

Enjoy games about Canada, its geography, and animals.

Justin Trudeau, Prime Minister of Canada Website

pm.gc.ca/eng

Visit the official website for Justin Trudeau, prime minister of Canada. Read about his life, see photos and videos, and learn news about the prime minister.

National Geographic Kids

kids.nationalgeographic.com/explore/countries/canada/#canada-playing-hockey.jpg

Learn about Canada, its people, culture, government, and history.

INDEX

Published in 2019 by Enslow Publishing, LLC.
101 W. 23rd Street, Suite 240, New York, NY 10011

Copyright © 2019 by Enslow Publishing, LLC.
All rights reserved.

No part of this book may be reproduced by any means without the written permission of the publisher.

Library of Congress Cataloging-in-Publication Data
Names: Furgang, Kathy, author.
Title: Justin Trudeau : prime minister of Canada / Kathy Furgang.
Description: New York : Enslow Publishing, 2019. | Series: Junior biographies | Includes bibliographical references and index. | Audience: Grade: 3 to 6. | Identifiers: LCCN 2017051705| ISBN 9780766097438 (library bound) | ISBN9780766097445 (pbk.) | ISBN 9780766097452 (6 pack)
Subjects: LCSH: Trudeau, Justin–Juvenile literature. | Prime ministers–Canada–Biography. | Canada–Politics and government–1980- |Liberal Party of Canada–Biography.
Classification: LCC F1034.3.T78 F87 2018 | DDC 971.07/4092 [B] –dc23
LC record available at https://lccn.loc.gov/2017051705

Printed in the United States of America

To Our Readers: We have done our best to make sure all website addresses in this book were active and appropriate when we went to press. However, the author and the publisher have no control over and assume no liability for the material available on those websites or on any websites they may link to. Any comments or suggestions can be sent by e-mail to customerservice@enslow.com.

Photos Credits: Cover, p. 1 Ilya S. Savenok/Getty Images; p. 4 Hector Vivas/LatinContent WO/Getty Images; p. 6 Boris Spremo/Toronto Star/Getty Images; p. 7 Bettmann/Getty Images; p. 9 Bernard Weil/Toronto Star/Getty Images; p. 10 David Boily/AFP/Getty Images; pp. 13, 14 Geoff Robins/AFP/Getty Images; p. 16 Anadolu Agency/Getty Images; p. 18 Andrew Chin/Getty Images; p. 20 AFP Contributor/AFP/Getty Images; p. 21 © AP Images; back cover, pp. 2, 3, 22, 23, 24 (curves graphic) Alena Kazlouskaya/Shutterstock.com; interior page bottoms (Canadian flag) patrice6000/Shutterstock.com.